Publish That Book Now Planner

Julia A. Royston

BA, MA, MLS, DRE

ROYSTON
Publishing

BK Royston Publishing

P. O. Box 4321

Jeffersonville, IN 47131

502-802-5385

http://www.bkroystonpublishing.com

bkroystonpublishing@gmail.com

Cover Design: Gad Savage, Elite Covers

ISBN-13: 978-1-951941-72-7

Printed in the United States of America

Dedication

To anyone who has ever wanted to publish a book but needed a plan.

Let's go!

Acknowledgements

First, I acknowledge my Lord and Savior Jesus Christ for giving me all of my gifts and especially my gift to write His words.

My husband who is always supportive, loving and encouraging me to utilize all of my gifts and talents. Thank you honey.

To my mother, Dr. Daisy Foree, who is my number one cheerleader and always tells me, "hang in there, you can do it." To my father, Dr. Jack Foree, who is never far away from me in spirit or my heart. I only have to look in the mirror each day to see him.

To Rev. Claude and Mrs. Lillie Royston, Michael and Jean Royston who support me in everything I do.

To the rest of my family, I love you and thank you for your prayers, support and love.

To My Business Bestie Vanessa Collins and all of the other "Business Queens" in the virtual and global world. I dedicate this to you. We work long and hard each day. I pray that you are profitable and prosperous in whatever business that you are pursuing. Blessings.

Table of Contents

Introduction

I wish I had some miraculous way and formula to give you for the 50+ books that I've written or the 300+ books I've published and helped others to publish. The secret is in the doing. You just have to do it. But, also you have to plan it out, set yourself up on a schedule and stick to it. Otherwise, in a year you still won't have the rough draft done and the book ready to go to the publisher.

In this book, I want to point out the six books that you should consider publishing, provide you with blank calendars to plan it out as well as give you some guidance along the way.

If you still have questions, don't hesitate to reach out to me at www.connectwithroyston.com to schedule a conversation regarding planning and publishing your next book.

Connect with me on social media at:

Facebook, Instagram and LinkedIN - @juliaaroyston

Twitter - @juliaakroyston

TikTok - @juliaroyston

Book

Prior to beginning the work in the Publish that Book Now Planner, I hope that you have purchased the accompanying book "Publish that Book Now." It will make more sense to read that book because it will then make more sense to be able to answer the question of what type of book you want to write and then complete the outline in this Planner regarding creating and writing your book.

If you have any questions, don't hesitate to reach out to us at www.connectwithroyston.com.

What type of book do you want to write?

_____
_____
_____
_____
_____
_____
_____
_____
_____
_____
_____
_____
_____
_____
_____

A Book doesn't have to be long to be strong but I admonish you to have an outline so that your writing is focused, precise, clear and will allow you to complete the book much faster than without an outline.

Book Outline

Topic of Your Book

_____
_____
_____

Subtopic 1

_____
_____
_____

Subtopic 2

_____
_____
_____

Subtopic 3

_____
_____
_____

Subtopic 4

_____
_____
_____

Subtopic 5

_____

_____

_____

Subtopic 6

_____

_____

_____

Subtopic 7

_____

_____

_____

Subtopic 8

_____

_____

_____

Subtopic 9

_____

_____

_____

Subtopic 10

_____

_____

_____

Now that you have the outline, begin writing about the topics on the outline. So, if you are writing about apples, start with the history of apples and continue down the outline under each section of the book.

Fill in the text under each topic. It's just that simple.

An outline is a great guide and map to writing your book. Once you are finished filling in the blanks or writing the text under your outline topics, go back and read what you have written. It will surprise you how much you have written. These topics can now be transposed into chapter titles. You could leave the chapter titles as simple as one-word headings or adjust them to longer sentences later. It is your choice. For more help with writing your book, reach out to us at http://www.connectwithroyston.com.

Why a Calendar?

There is something about putting a date on something that makes it a goal, gives it a target due date and creates a sense of urgency for the project to be completed. I am a planner by nature and hoping to give you a valuable tool that I use each and every day which is a calendar. I mark, circle, type in my phone and share with my team when things are due to keep us on track to produce the next product. We can meet the needs of our client with products that we haven't produced yet. We can profit from a product that hasn't been produced yet. So, on the next page is one of the vital tools that I use to make our business as productive as possible, a calendar. I left it blank purposely because I want you to set the date of when you want to complete a specific product. My timelines are not your timelines and vice versa.

SUN	MON	TUE	WED	THU	FRI	SAT

Notes

_____
_____
_____
_____
_____
_____
_____
_____
_____
_____
_____
_____
_____
_____
_____
_____
_____
_____
_____
_____
_____
_____
_____
_____
_____
_____

**PUBLISH THAT
BOOK NOW
PLANNER**
#connectwithroyston

eBook

Prior to beginning the work in the Publish That Book Now Planner, I hope that you have purchased the accompanying book "Publish That Book Now." It will make more sense and then complete the outline in this Planner regarding creating and writing your eBook. If you have any questions, don't hesitate to reach out to us at bkroystonpublishing@gmail.com.

What topic will you write about in an eBook? The number of pages can be from 5-10. What will you talk about?

_____
_____
_____
_____
_____
_____
_____
_____
_____
_____
_____
_____
_____
_____
_____
_____

Just because an eBook may be shorter doesn't mean that it is not as impactful as a full-length book. Full length books should be available in print and eBook format. If you are beginning the process of writing your first book, you may consider writing an eBook first. Extend the eBook so that it can be printed and available in paperback and electronic format. I don't suggest one or the other but have both formats. For more help with writing your book, reach out to us at http://www.talkwithroyston.com.

eBook Outline

Topic of Your Book

_____

_____

_____

Subtopic 1

_____

_____

_____

Subtopic 2

_____

_____

Subtopic 3

_____

_____

Subtopic 4

_____

_____

_____

Subtopic 5

_____

_____

_____

WHEN WILL YOU START?

bkroystonpublishing@gmail.com
www.bkroystonstore.com

Be sure and mark the calendar on the next page of when you want your eBook to be completed. Let's go!

SUN	MON	TUE	WED	THU	FRI	SAT

Notes

_____
_____
_____
_____
_____
_____
_____
_____
_____
_____
_____
_____
_____
_____
_____
_____
_____
_____
_____
_____
_____
_____
_____

**PUBLISH THAT
BOOK NOW
PLANNER**

#connectwithroyston

Notes

_____
_____
_____
_____
_____
_____
_____
_____
_____
_____
_____
_____
_____
_____
_____
_____
_____
_____
_____
_____
_____
_____

**PUBLISH THAT
BOOK NOW
PLANNER**
#connectwithroyston

Audiobook

Prior to beginning the work in the Publish That Book Now Planner, I hope that you have purchased the accompanying book "Publish That Book Now." It will make more sense and then read my short article on the things to consider prior to beginning an Audiobook. Review your book that you are considering for an audiobook, put a date on the calendar regarding creating your Audiobook and then reach out to us for the next steps to begin the audiobook process.

If you have any questions, don't hesitate to email us at bkroystonpublishing@gmail.com.

Things to Consider Prior to Beginning the Audiobook Process

You may be an author with a print or eBook and hopefully, both, who is now ready to explore the audiobook world. I want you to take time out to consider some things prior to jumping right in. Counting up the cost is not just about money but the audiobook world has different players, rules and payment plans along with the new format.

Audiobook services are a subscription service. Why is that important to know? They already have an audience. They wish to grow their audience and continue to receive the monthly subscription fees. Thus, they demand the highest quality audio materials to be added to their database.

Audiobooks are reviewed, critiqued and chosen prior to being added to an audiobook service. Just because you have finished the book doesn't automatically mean that it will be accepted.

Best Books for Audiobooks are non-fiction (that doesn't rely on pictures, images or graphics to convey the message), fiction, children's chapter books and not picture books or children's books with illustrations and poetry works best.

Reviews of your print or eBook. Did people like your book? That's a hard question to ask and as an author and artist, I am as sensitive about my work as any ne but you need to be honest and determine the reviews and comments regarding your book before beginning the audiobook process.

Finished, Final and edited Book – It does matter the length of the book for audiobooks. In my opinion, it needs to be a 7-10 complete chapter book at the least. Before beginning the audiobook process, it needs to be finished. We can review it and determine the editing necessary and let you know that cost. If it is not finished, do not start the audiobook process. Finish the book, then reach out to us regarding the audiobook process.

Audiobooks are an investment. I mean an investment of time as much as money. Marketing and promotion are just as or more important with audiobooks as they are with the print book. The audiobook promotional plan has to be with the virtual, digital and internet world rather than the physical world although you should consider having physical copies of the audiobooks as well. Not a lot but some for the older generation who are not as computer savvy.

No exclusivity with Audiobooks. I have control issues and I would not be exclusive with one service. I would be willing to take less royalties from one service and have the ability to launch my book with multiple services as well as my own website, rather than to only be able to get royalties from one audiobook service. If you are ready for the next level, connect with us via email at bkroystonpublishing@gmail.com or schedule a free consultation at http://www.connectwithroyston.com

To preview my audiobooks, visit http://www.amazon.com and type in "The Gifted" and Julia Royston. Enjoy! Any questions, reach out.

What type of book have your written that can be easily be turned into an audiobook?

_____
_____
_____
_____
_____
_____
_____
_____
_____
_____

Do you have empowerment quotes or social media posts that you do daily that can be easily and quickly transferred to audio?

_____
_____
_____
_____
_____
_____
_____
_____
_____
_____
_____
_____

WHEN WILL YOU START?

bkroystonpublishing@gmail.com
www.bkroystonstore.com

Use the calendar on the next page to either schedule a time for us to talk or when you want the audiobook completed. Due dates move your feet and push you toward completion.

SUN	MON	TUE	WED	THU	FRI	SAT

Notes

_____
_____
_____
_____
_____
_____
_____
_____
_____
_____
_____
_____
_____
_____
_____
_____
_____
_____
_____
_____
_____
_____
_____
_____
_____
_____
_____

**PUBLISH THAT
BOOK NOW
PLANNER**

#connectwithroyston

Workbook

Prior to beginning the work in the Publish That Book Now Planner, I hope that you have purchased the accompanying book "Publish That Book Now." It will make more sense and then review the short article below regarding 5 reasons why you should create workbook.

Next what are some things that you want to include in the workbook that wasn't in the original book? Begin creating the additional documents and activities that you want to include in the workbook.

Put a date on the calendar regarding creating your workbook and then reach out to us if you have any questions, via email at bkroystonpublishing@gmail.com.

Why create a workbook?

When we were growing up, we were told that you shouldn't write in a book. This is true with other books but a workbook is designed especially for writing, planning and organizing your thoughts, ideas and next steps.

1. **A workbook is an actual working document.** Similar to a playbook, manual or other guide book, a workbook will help you work through a process to complete a project or produce a product.
2. **There are worksheets or documents that actually need to be completed**. With real estate, financial planning and other more involved projects, there are worksheets, survey and checklists that may need to be completed before beginning a project. These documents can easily be compiled in a workbook to make sure that the client or customer has everything that need in one place.

3. **A workbook accompanies the main book**. Thus, it is an additional product for sale and purchase. More products equal more profits.
4. **Customer Education**. The workbook is a helpful tool and resource to educate your client and/or customer in the vocabulary, terminology and processes within your industry and business.
5. **Lead Generation**. When you provide high quality products, services and experiences for customers, they normally want to do more business with you than initially expected. A workbook can become an invaluable tool and also if contact information is provided inside, continue to be a source and resource for future endeavors and projects.

What do you need to include in your workbook?

- Handouts
- History of Organization
- Activities
- Upcoming Events
- Website
- Locations
- Contact Information
- Surveys
- Spreadsheets
- Checklists
- Worksheets
- Diagrams
- Images
- Glossary of Terms
- List of Non-Profit Organizations
- Helpline
- Support Groups/Organizations
- Governmental Entities for Assistance
- Index of Resources

A general layout in your workbook is similar to this book that you are reviewing.

Refer to the main book's information and reference the page number and/or chapter for the basis of the activities included in your workbook.

Discussion Questions

Forms

Handouts

Activities

In case of an emergency or need help, contact us at this phone, email or web address.

If you have any questions, don't hesitate to reach out to us at bkroystonpublishing@gmail.com or schedule an appointment at http://www.connectwithroyston.com

Here are some examples of workbooks that I have created in the past as a guide to help you as you create your workbook.

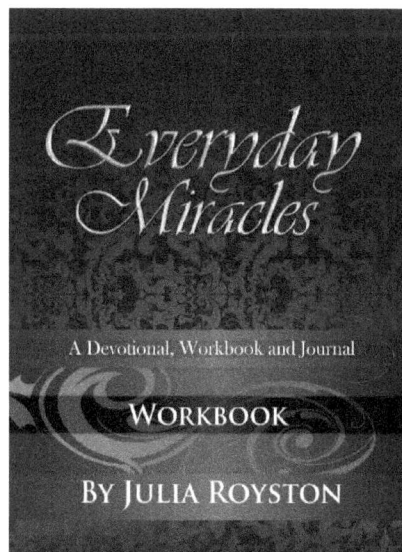

WHEN WILL YOU START?

bkroystonpublishing@gmail.com
www.bkroystonstore.com

It's time to put a due date on completion of your workbook. See on the next page, a blank calendar that you can determine when you will be ready to release your industry and content rich workbook.

SUN	MON	TUE	WED	THU	FRI	SAT

Notes

_____
_____
_____
_____
_____
_____
_____
_____
_____
_____
_____
_____
_____
_____
_____
_____
_____
_____
_____
_____
_____
_____
_____
_____
_____
_____

**PUBLISH THAT
BOOK NOW
PLANNER**

#connectwithroyston

Planner/Checklist

Prior to beginning the work in the Publish That Book Now Planner, I hope that you have purchased the accompanying book "Publish that Book Now."

Next what are some things that you want to include in your planner and on your checklist. You may consider having checklists inside your planner.

Planners are great for scheduling, preparing for upcoming events and/or creating additional products and services.

So, some questions to ask yourself:

Who is this planner for?

_____
_____
_____
_____
_____
_____
_____

What are planning for and what would the layout be for this planner?

_____
_____
_____
_____
_____

_____
_____

The format for the planner can be determined later but begin to look at different sizes, binding and layouts of planners. Which type of planner do you like is not as important as the format of the planner for the clients and/or customers that you are striving to attract?

What type of information is needed for a helpful business checklist?

_____
_____
_____
_____
_____
_____
_____
_____
_____

My ultimate business checklist should include

_____
_____
_____
_____
_____
_____
_____
_____
_____
_____
_____
_____
_____
_____
_____

_____

_____

_____

WHEN WILL YOU START?

bkroystonpublishing@gmail.com
www.bkroystonstore.com

Put a date on the calendar regarding creating your planner/checklist and then reach out to us if you have any questions, via email at bkroystonpublishing@gmail.com.

SUN	MON	TUE	WED	THU	FRI	SAT

Notes

_____
_____
_____
_____
_____
_____
_____
_____
_____
_____
_____
_____
_____
_____
_____
_____
_____
_____
_____
_____
_____
_____

**PUBLISH THAT
BOOK NOW
PLANNER**

#connectwithroyston

Notes

_____
_____
_____
_____
_____
_____
_____
_____
_____
_____
_____
_____
_____
_____
_____
_____
_____
_____
_____
_____
_____
_____

**PUBLISH THAT
BOOK NOW
PLANNER**

#connectwithroyston

Journal

Prior to beginning the work in the Publish That Book Now Planner, I hope that you have purchased the accompanying book "Publish That Book Now."

Next what are some things that you want to include in your journal.

Journals can be used as a very therapeutic tool. They are similar to the traditional diaries but can be used for writing down your thoughts, creating action steps for major projects as well as keeping record of your daily tasks and events.

What type of Journal do you need to create for your business?

_____

_____

_____

_____

_____

_____

_____

_____

_____

_____

_____

_____

_____

_____

Some examples of journals created have been used especially with inspirational and motivational books. Journals can also be used with business and other non-fiction book topics.

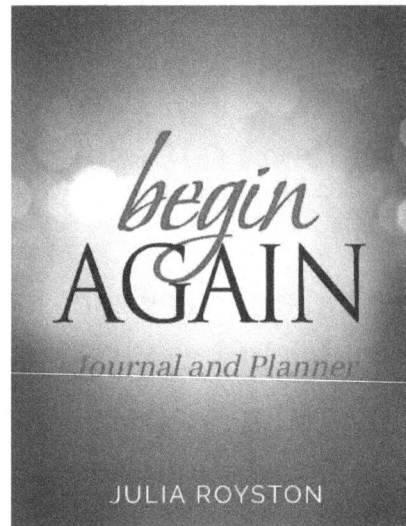

WHEN WILL YOU START?

bkroystonpublishing@gmail.com
www.bkroystonstore.com

Put a date on the calendar regarding creating your Journal and then reach out to us if you have any questions, via email at bkroystonpublishing@gmail.com.

SUN	MON	TUE	WED	THU	FRI	SAT

Notes

_____
_____
_____
_____
_____
_____
_____
_____
_____
_____
_____
_____
_____
_____
_____
_____
_____
_____
_____
_____
_____
_____
_____

**PUBLISH THAT
BOOK NOW
PLANNER**

#connectwithroyston

After you've published one of these books, I am certain you will want to publish more. Below are 12 more blank calendars so that you can plan what you will publish next as well as some additional blank pages so that you can not miss a thing. Remember, if you need help, visit www.connectwithroyston.com to schedule a consultation. Let's go!

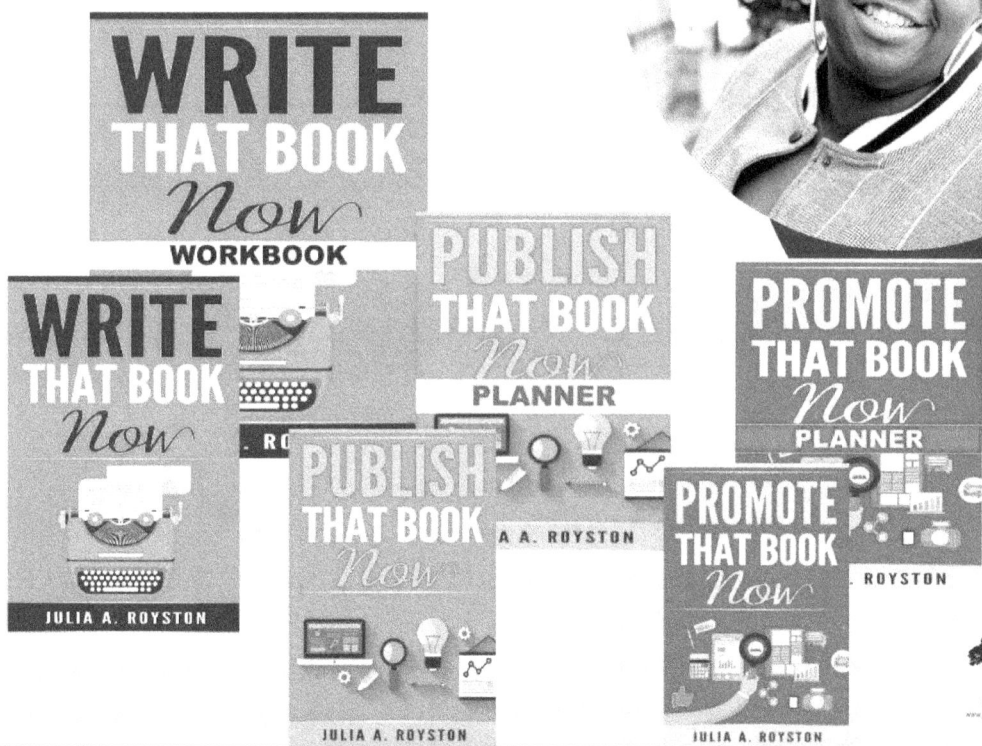

SUN	MON	TUE	WED	THU	FRI	SAT

SUN	MON	TUE	WED	THU	FRI	SAT

SUN	MON	TUE	WED	THU	FRI	SAT

SUN	MON	TUE	WED	THU	FRI	SAT

SUN	MON	TUE	WED	THU	FRI	SAT

SUN	MON	TUE	WED	THU	FRI	SAT

SUN	MON	TUE	WED	THU	FRI	SAT

SUN	MON	TUE	WED	THU	FRI	SAT

SUN	MON	TUE	WED	THU	FRI	SAT

SUN	MON	TUE	WED	THU	FRI	SAT

SUN	MON	TUE	WED	THU	FRI	SAT

SUN	MON	TUE	WED	THU	FRI	SAT

Notes

_____
_____
_____
_____
_____
_____
_____
_____
_____
_____
_____
_____
_____
_____
_____
_____
_____
_____
_____
_____
_____
_____
_____
_____
_____

**PUBLISH THAT
BOOK NOW
PLANNER**

#connectwithroyston

Notes

_____
_____
_____
_____
_____
_____
_____
_____
_____
_____
_____
_____
_____
_____
_____
_____
_____
_____
_____
_____
_____
_____
_____

**PUBLISH THAT
BOOK NOW
PLANNER**

#connectwithroyston

Notes

_____
_____
_____
_____
_____
_____
_____
_____
_____
_____
_____
_____
_____
_____
_____
_____
_____
_____
_____
_____
_____
_____
_____
_____
_____
_____

**PUBLISH THAT
BOOK NOW
PLANNER**

#connectwithroyston

Notes

_____
_____
_____
_____
_____
_____
_____
_____
_____
_____
_____
_____
_____
_____
_____
_____
_____
_____
_____
_____
_____
_____
_____
_____
_____

**PUBLISH THAT
BOOK NOW
PLANNER**

#connectwithroyston

Notes

_____
_____
_____
_____
_____
_____
_____
_____
_____
_____
_____
_____
_____
_____
_____
_____
_____
_____
_____
_____
_____
_____
_____
_____

**PUBLISH THAT
BOOK NOW
PLANNER**

#connectwithroyston

Notes

PUBLISH THAT
BOOK NOW
PLANNER

#connectwithroyston

Notes

_____
_____
_____
_____
_____
_____
_____
_____
_____
_____
_____
_____
_____
_____
_____
_____
_____
_____
_____
_____
_____
_____
_____
_____

**PUBLISH THAT
BOOK NOW
PLANNER**
#connectwithroyston

About the Author

Julia Royston spend her days doing what she loves, writing, publishing, speaking and coaching others to tell, introduce and create ways to deliver their stories and messages to the world. That is her "Why." BK Royston Publishing LLC, Julia Royston.net, Royal Media and Publishing and Royston Book Fairs are the conduits that she and her husband, Brian Royston use to spread the love of reading, writing, books as well as build businesses around the world. To date, Julia has written 50+ books, recorded 3 music CDs and Coached 150+ to write and publish books as well as established their own businesses.

Julia is currently the host of "Live Your Best Life" a Weekly Podcast and Broadcast that highlights guests with resourceful information, inspiration and empowerment to help people to live their best life brought to you by BK Royston Publishing.

Follow her on social media or visit www.bkroystonpublishing.com or www.juliaroyston.net for more information and upcoming events.